SUNSHINE

BY HARRIET BRUNDLE

Weather
Explorers

Weather
Explorers

©2016
Book Life
King's Lynn
Norfolk
PE30 4LS

ISBN: 978-1-910512-72-2

Written by:
Harriet Brundle
Edited by:
Gemma McMullen
Designed by:
Ian McMullen

A catalogue record for this book
is available from the British Library.

CONTENTS

Words in **bold** can be found in the glossary on page 24.

SUNSHINE

When the sun is shining, the weather feels warm.

°C °F

50 — 120

40 — 100

30 — 80

20 — 60

10 — 40

0 — 20

10 — 0

20 — 20

30

A THERMOMETER

We measure how warm it is outside by using a thermometer.

WHAT IS THE SUN?

GASES

The sun is a star. It is made from gases that are very hot.

The sun is many **miles** away from Earth but its heat is so powerful it lights and warms our planet.

EARTH

SUN

WITHOUT THE SUN, OUR PLANET WOULD BE DARK AND COLD.

SEASONS OF THE YEAR

There are four seasons in a year.

SPRING

SUMMER

WINTER

AUTUMN

8

The summer months are June, July and August.

SUNNY SUMMER

Summer is the warmest season.
The sun seems brightest in the summer.

There are more hours of daylight in summer than in any other season.

WHAT DO WE WEAR?

T-SHIRT

SHORTS

When the sun is shining, we need to stay cool. We wear t-shirts and shorts.

It is important to wear a hat to **protect** our head from the sun.

TOO MUCH SUNSHINE CAN MAKE US FEEL UNWELL.

PLANTS

Plants need sunlight so that they can grow bigger.

14

We need to water plants ourselves when the sun is shining as there is no rain.

WATERING

ANIMALS

There is lots of food for animals to eat in the summertime.

Some animals **shed** part of their fur when the weather is warm. This helps them to keep cool.

FUN IN THE SUN

It is fun to go to the seaside when the sun is shining.

We can go for an outdoor picnic in warm weather.

DID YOU KNOW?

There are some places in the world where the sun doesn't stop shining for six whole months. The sun even shines at night time!

Deserts are places where the weather is very hot. Very few plants and animals can **survive** in the desert.

CACTUS

BEING SAFE IN THE SUN

It is not safe to look straight at the sun, even when wearing dark glasses.

BE CAREFUL, IT WILL HURT YOUR EYES!

The sun can burn our skin, so it is important to put on sun cream for **protection**.

GLOSSARY

Miles: a measure of distance.

Protect/Protection: keeping something safe from something else.

Shed: when something falls out or drops off.

Survive: stay alive.

CREDITS

Photocredits: Abbreviations: l-left, r-right, b-bottom, t-top, c-centre, m-middle. All images are courtesy of Shutterstock.com.

Front Cover – Elenamiv. 1 – Oksana Shufrych. 2-3 – vvita. 4 – AlinaMD. 5 ChameleonsEye. 6 – Markus Gann. 7 – Triff. 8tl – Drew Rawcliffe. 8tr – Sunny studio. 8bl – Steve Horsley. 8br – balounm. 9 – JonesHon. 10 – MarKord. 11 – altanaka. 12 – karelnoppe. 13 – Aleksei Potov. 13inset – Piotr Wawrzyniuk. 14 – Patrick Foto. 15 – Studio 37. 16 – Dudarev Mikhail. 16inset – Subbotina Anna. 17 – DreamBig. 18 – krutar. 19 – EmiliaUngur. 20 – Enrico Maniscalco. 21 – Paul Matthew Photography. 22 – YanLev. 23 – MarKord. 24 – samarttiw.